PLAY·THE·GAME

ICE

HOCKEY

Ian Brace·

WARD LOCK

First published in 1990 by Ward Lock.
This revised edition published 1995 by
Blandford, an imprint of the Cassell Group,
Wellington House, 125 Strand, London
WC2R 0BB

Reprinted 1998

Illustrations by Jerry Malone

Printed and bound in Great Britain
by The Bath Press, Bath

British Library Cataloguing in Publication Data

ISBN 0 7137 2517 6

Acknowledgments

The author and publishers would like to
thank Mike Smith and Bruce Bennett for
supplying all photographs in this book, with
the exception of p. 2 (frontispiece), supplied
by Colorsport, and David Pickles for his help
in revising the book for this new edition.

**Frontispiece: Wayne Gretzky, one of the
finest hockey players of all time**

ICE
HOCKEY

CONTENTS

FOREWORD

I was delighted to accept the publisher's invitation to write a foreword to this publication.

The author, Ian Brace, has drawn in his information from far and wide and has prepared a publication which embraces the wide concepts of our sport.

The book starts with the development of the game, especially our glorious pre-war years, and goes farther back to the unusual origins of the sport. There is emphasis placed on great leagues and teams and on our own early leagues and teams. This history comes quickly up to date,

encompassing the growth of the sport both in this country and abroad.

The reader is guided diligently through the rink dimensions and markings and player's equipment is mentioned.

The advice on tactics and techniques is made very clear and presented in a simple manner along with excellent diagrams and illustrations.

The complex penalty structure and disciplinary code is well detailed in an informative but interesting manner. The do's and don't's have been clearly defined.

The terminology section is commendable for sensible unravelling of what to most people is almost a 'slang' talk, and explains clearly the game's phrases. The Rules Clinic will cause even the experts in our sport to dive to their rule books but the author is spot on with his question and answer section and has certainly read the rule book from cover to cover.

The illustrations and diagrams activate the rules in an interesting and informative manner.

This book is written with the player in mind, and both the players themselves and their coaches will gain a great deal from the information and knowledge given in the text and diagrams.

This publication is a vital addition to our sport's library and everyone at the British Ice Hockey Association is grateful to Ian Brace for writing *Play the Game: Ice Hockey*.

David Pickles
General Secretary
British Ice Hockey Association

Sheffield Steelers' Dean Smith (centre) challenges the Romford Raider goalie Brian Cox

HISTORY &

DEVELOPMENT OF

ICE HOCKEY

Unquestionably the world's fastest team game, with its participants reaching speeds of 35mph, and the puck three times that fast, its speed and the extreme skill of the players help make ice hockey one of the most exciting games in the world to both play and watch.

The ability of the heavily padded players to display such bursts of speed, stops, turns, and outstanding stick movement, demands the utmost of respect from ice hockey fans the world over.

Whilst Canada and the United States are hotbeds of ice hockey, it has many European connections and Czechoslovakia and the Soviet Union are outstanding nations at international level. In Britain, the sport enjoyed a period of popularity in the inter-war years and in 1936 Britain was the surprise Olympic, World and European champion. Sadly, the game declined in Britain but in recent years there has been a huge upsurge in popularity of ice hockey, particularly in the number of youngsters taking up the sport, and organized games attract large crowds to the ice rinks up and down Britain each weekend during the season. Emphasis is now placed on the

sport being a family game as more women and children take it up. Ice hockey may not figure among the top five sports in Britain, as it does in North America, but it is certainly making steady progress up the sporting ladder.

But where did it all start, and when?

Well, ice hockey is yet another of the many sports which cannot pinpoint its exact roots. Let's face it, somebody, somewhere, in the mists of time must have stood on a piece of ice with a stick in their hand and hit a stone. That, for all intent and purpose, would have been the forerunner of ice hockey, although they wouldn't have known it at the time.

Canada claims to be the birthplace of ice hockey as a sport. But that is where the arguments rage. Several Canadian cities claim to have been the first to play the game, notably Kingston (Ontario), and Montreal. Certainly the claim that it was first played at Kingston is a valid one – it was played by Crimea War veterans from the Royal Canadian Rifles who played 'field' hockey on Kingston harbour when it was frozen over in 1860. But instead of using a ball they used a puck. It was the first time a puck was used and thus gave the 'new' sport its own dentity. British troops also played hockey on ice in Nova Scotia around the same time.

Montreal's claim on ice hockey's birthright came in 1879 when WF Robertson and RF Smith, students at the city's McGill University, formulated the first set of rules, which were a cross between field hockey and rugby rules! Their early rules dictated the use of a square rubber puck and teams of nine players.

Robertson had visited England to watch field hockey with the intention of adapting some of its rules to the new game on ice.

In 1880 the first recognized hockey team, the McGill University Hockey Club, was formed, thus strengthening Montreal's rightful claim to the sport. Five years later, a member of the McGill team, AP Low, introduced the game to Ottawa.

Shortly after the formation of the McGill club, other teams were formed and leagues soon spread throughout Canada. By the time the first club was formed in the United States, in 1893, there were nearly one hundred clubs in the Montreal area. The first game in the United States was between Yale University and Johns Hopkins University in Baltimore.

In the same year that ice hockey came to the United States, Lord Stanley of Preston, the Governor-General of Canada donated the Stanley Cup to be played for annually. The Montreal Amateur Athletic Association became the first winners in 1894 when they beat the Ottawa Capitals 3–1 in front of a crowd of 5,000 spectators. The Stanley Cup has since gone on to become the sport's most famous trophy.

Hockey fever soon gripped the United States and at New York in 1896 the United States Amateur Hockey League was founded. By the start of the twentieth century, ice hockey was being played in Europe, largely owing to the efforts of a Canadian team touring Britain and a five-nation tournament, also played in Britain, in 1903.

However, this was nothing new to Britain.

Hockey on ice had been played in England at the end of the nineteenth century, notably at Wimbledon Common. In 1895 there was a famous match on the lake in the grounds of Buckingham Palace when the Prince of Wales and the Duke of York, who both later became Kings of England (Edward VII and George V), were in a Palace team which played a Lord Stanley team. The result was reported as: 'Numerous goals for the Stanley team to the single goal of the Palace side.'

The International Ice Hockey Federation (IIHF) was formed in 1908 and the founder members were Belgium, Bohemia, France, Great Britain and Switzerland. Two years later, Great Britain won the first European Ice Hockey Championship, played at Les Avants in the Swiss Alps. Surprisingly, however, the British Ice Hockey association was not formed until four years after their triumph. The five founder-member clubs of the British association were Cambridge, Manchester, Oxford Canadians, Royal Engineers, and Princes.

A world and Olympic championship was first held in 1920, when Canada won both titles at the 1920 Olympics. A separate world championship was not instituted until 1930.

In the period between the two world wars,

ice hockey became extremely popular in Britain as a spectator sport. This development coincided with the increase in electrically frozen rinks, notably at Westminster in 1926, the Empire Pool, Wembley, in 1924, the Brighton Sports Stadium, Haringay Arena, and London's Empress Hall. An influx of Canadian players into the British game improved the standard of play considerably, and by 1936 Britain was a world force at international level. Then came that surprise Olympic gold medal at Garmisch when the British team beat Canada 2–1 and held the United States to a goal-less draw. Until then, the Canadians had won every Olympic tournament, and only once, in 1933, lost their world title, to the United States. Now they had lost both titles to the unlikely British team. It was a major upset.

On the domestic front, the British game was dominated by such teams as Wembley Lions, Richmond Hawks, Wembley Canadians, and the truly outstanding team of the era, Streatham.

Sadly, after the Second World War the game declined in Britain largely because of the shortage of rinks big enough to stage matches, or large enough to hold the spectators. But while ice hockey's demise was seen in Britain, the sport continued to flourish elsewhere. Perhaps understandably, Nordic nations like Sweden and Finland became forces to be reckoned with at international level, but so did the mighty Soviets and their neighbours, Czechoslovakia. Today, ice hockey is a truly international sport, with diverse nations such as North and South Korea, India, Australia and Greece competing alongside the more established North American and European teams.

But, for organized ice hockey at the highest level, one has to look at the National Hockey League (NHL) in Canada and the United States. It is the sport's major professional league and brings together the leading 21 teams in North America each year.

The first all-professional club in North America was the Portlage Lake club in Michigan, which was formed in 1903, although individual professionals had been playing in Canada before then. The first professional league was the International Hockey League, which operated in northern Michigan between 1904 and 1906. The first fully professional league was formed in Ontario in 1908.

Until 1910, professionals and amateurs were allowed to play together on 'mixed teams', but this ended when the first major professional league, the National Hockey Association (NHA), was founded in eastern Canada in 1910. Hockey on the west coast was played under the auspices of the Pacific Coast League, which was formed a year later.

Seattle and other American cities joined the NHA and the Stanley Cup, which was previously contested by 'mixed' teams, became the trophy awarded to winners of the professional league play offs.

The National Hockey League (NHL) was inaugurated in its present form in 1917 following a meeting at Montreal, and it replaced the NHA.

Only four teams contested the league in its first season; the Wanderers and Canadiens from Montreal, the Ottawa Senators, and the Toronto Arenas, who became the first

Referee Andy Carson manages to avoid the action of the challenge between Les Millie and Chuck Taylor

League champions. They were later to become the Toronto Maple Leafs, one of the most famous names in the NHL. The Boston Bruins became the first American team to join the NHL, in 1924.

By 1943 the league had settled down to a membership of the 'Big Six': the Boston Bruins, Chicago Black Hawks, Detroit Red Wings, Montreal Canadiens, New York Rangers and Toronto Maple Leafs. The champions received the Prince of Wales Trophy and the leading four teams each year contested the post-season playoffs for the Stanley Cup.

However, increased interest among potential franchisees brought about an increase in the number of professional teams over the next quarter of a century and in the 1967–68 season the league was expanded to 12 teams with the addition of the Los Angeles Kings, Minnesota North Stars, Oakland Seals, Philadelphia Flyers, Pittsburgh Penguins and St Louis Blues. Because of the increased number of clubs, the newcomers formed a Western Division, while the existing clubs became the Eastern Division.

At the time of the formation of the two divisions, the longest-serving member of the NHL was Gordie Howe, who had first started playing for the Red Wings in 1946. He was regarded as the finest player of all time and scored a record 1,850 points by the time he retired in 1971. His record stood for 18 years until it was surpassed by the finest present-day player, Wayne Gretzky, who was traded from the Edmonton Oilers to the Los Angeles Kings for a staggering $15 million in 1988.

Today, the 21 teams of the NHL are divided into two Conferences, the Wales Conference and the Campbell Conference. Each conference has two divisions. The Wales Conference divisions are known as the Patrick and Adams Divisions, and the Campbell Conference is split into the Norris and Smythe Divisions – they are all named after famous hockey owners of the past.

The teams in the NHL in 1989–90 were:

EASTERN CONFERENCE: Atlantic Division: Washington Capitals, New York Rangers, Philadelphia Flyers, New Jersey Devils, New York Islanders, Florida Panthers, Tampa Bay Lightning.

EASTERN CONFERENCE; North East Division: Montreal Canadiens, Boston Bruins, Buffalo Sabres, Hartford Whalers, Quebec Nordiques, Pittsburgh Penguins, Ottawa Senators.

WESTERN CONFERENCE; Central Division, Detroit Red Wings, St Louis Blues, Chicago Black Hawks, Toronto Maple Leafs, Dallas Stars, Winnepeg Jets.

WESTERN CONFERENCE; Pacific Division: Calgary Flames, Los Angeles Kings, Edmonton Oilers, Vancouver Canucks, Anaheim Mighty Ducks, San Jose Sharks.

The NHL season lasts from October to May. After playing a total of 80 games in the regular season, the best teams in each Division enter the playoffs and the winners meet in their respective Conference finals. The two Conference winners then meet in the best-of-seven Stanley Cup final.

British ice hockey has enjoyed a great period of revival in the 1980s largely thanks to the financial support of Heineken, who lent their name to the British league, which was in existence from 1982 to 1993.

There are currently two divisions of the British League, the Premier Division and Division One. The English league has been the starting base for many of the luxury stadia, such as those in Bracknell and Basingstoke. The top British teams in recent years have included Murrayfield Racers, Durham Wasps, Fife Flyers, Nottingham Panthers, and more recently, Cardiff Devils.

Crowds are increasing all the time at British ice hockey arenas, and most weekends they are filled to capacity. It may never reach the popularity level of the NHL, but it is certainly one of Britain's most progressive sports. Those of you who have been to a live match won't need telling what an exciting game ice hockey is.

EQUIPMENT & TERMINOLOGY

Ice hockey is played on an electrically frozen ice rink by two teams, each consisting of not more than six players (usually, the goalkeeper, two defencemen and three forwards) on the ice at any one time. Each player wears specially designed skates and protective clothing. To propel the rubberized puck, he uses a stick with a larger head than a field hockey stick. Let's look at all ice hockey equipment in closer detail.

EQUIPMENT

The Rink

The rink should measure between 56 and 61m (60 and 66yd) long and 26 and 30m (28 and 33yd) wide. However, for International Ice Hockey Federation (IIHF) championship matches, these measurements are 60–61m (65–66yd) long and 29–30 (32–33yd) wide.

The rink should be surrounded by a wooden or plastic fence, known as the **boards**, which should be between 1.20 and 1.22m (3ft 9in and 4ft) above the surface of the ice. The entire playing area, and the boards, should be predominantly white. Any doors leading on to the ice must open inwards and not towards the playing area.

The four corners of the rink must be rounded in the arc of a circle with a radius of 7–8.5 m (23–28ft).

Because ice hockey is so fast, anybody hit with a puck travelling at speed is likely to receive a severe injury. That is why the players wear protective clothing. To protect the spectators most rinks have shatter-proof glass or perspex on top of the boards.

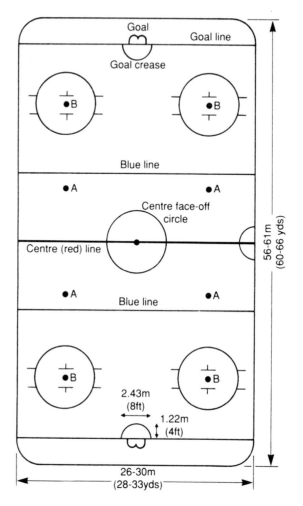

The playing area … the rink.

The goals

The goals are positioned 4m (13ft) from each end of the rink and at a central point on a 5cm (2in) red line drawn across the width of the ice and vertically up the side of the boards. They should remain stationary during a game.

The goals consist of two uprights and a crossbar made out of an approved material. The posts are 1.83m (6ft) apart, measured from the inside of the posts. And the cross

bar is 1.22m (4ft) above the surface of the ice.

A net is attached to the posts and its deepest point from the goal line should be between 60cm and 1.12m (2ft and 3ft 3in). The goal posts and crossbar should be painted red. The other supporting framework of the goals should be painted white. The red line across the rink on which the goal stands is known as the goal line.

*The rink, showing the boards and
protective area above them.*

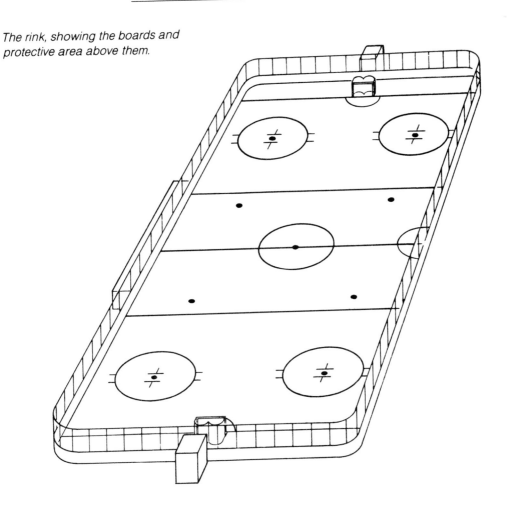

The rink's markings

Goal crease   A semi-circular area in front of
each goal, known as the crease, is drawn to a
radius of 180cm using the middle of the goal
line as its centre point. The area defined by the
goal crease is the space outlined by the crease
lines and extending vertically to a height of
1.22m (4ft); in other words, level with the top of
the goal.

   The lines used to define the goal crease are
red and measure 5cm (2in) wide.

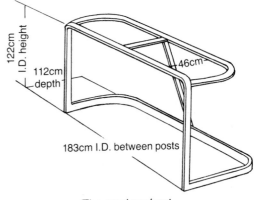

122cm
I.D. height

112cm
depth

46cm

183cm I.D. between posts

The goal and net.

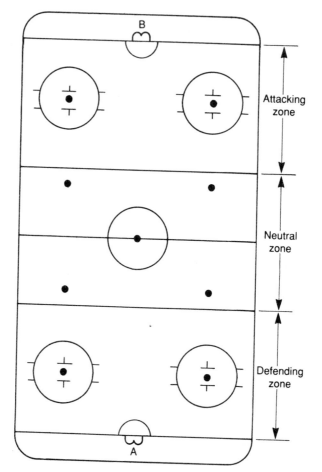

These are the three zones as seen from the team defending goal A. For the team defending the opposite goal, the attacking and defending zones are the other way around.

Division of ice surface   Vertical lines divide the playing surface into distinct areas.

We have already seen the position of the **goal lines.** Two other lines, each 30cm (12in) wide and blue in colour, divide the surface into three equal parts. These **blue lines**, like the goal lines, extend across the rink and vertically up the boards.

The three zones created by these two blue lines are (a) the **neutral zone** (the zone in the middle) and (b) the **attacking** and **defending**

zones. The zone in which a team's goal is situated is their defending zone while the zone furthest away from their goal is their attacking zone. Each of these zones is called an end zone.

A central line, called the **red line**, is drawn between the two blue lines. It is also 30cm (12in) wide and is painted red. It is drawn across the width of the rink, parallel to the goal lines and, again, extends vertically up the boards.

At the middle of the red, or centre, line a

centre spot is drawn. It is blue and measures 5cm (2in) in diameter. The centre of the spot is the centre of a circle with a 4.5m (5ft) radius, which is drawn in a blue line 5cm (2in) wide. This circle is the **centre circle** – what else would you really call it?

In the neutral zone there are four **face-off circles**, painted with red outlines and 60cm (2ft) in diameter. They are drawn 1.5m (5ft) from each blue line and 7m (23ft) from the centre of the rink. Within each face-off circle there is a centre spot, painted red, on which the referee drops the puck during a face-off.

There are two face-off circles in each end zone, one either side of the goal. The size of the spots are the same as those in the neutral zone and the radius of the circles is the same as the centre circle. The spots and lines defining the circles should be red.

Other ancillary equipment

Players' benches   These should be provided for up to 16 team members and six officials and access from them to the ice should be easy. The benches should be situated in the area behind the boards level with the neutral zone and as near to the centre of the rink as possible. Only players dressed for play, plus up to six officials from each team, are allowed on the bench at any one time.

The rink will also have a Penalty bench for each team adjacent to the neutral zone.

For players sent off the rink for a limited period a penalty bench must be provided. It should be well away from the normal players' bench, and ideally there should be a penalty bench for each team which should, for obvious reasons, also be well apart. The penalty benches must be situated in the neutral zone opposite the players' benches.

Timekeepers should be equipped with a suitable siren, or something similar, to indicate the end of the periods. And all rinks should have a conveniently placed clock so that spectators, officials and players can be kept informed of time remaining.

Because most ice hockey is played indoors it is important that the lighting be adequate for both players and spectators.

Playing equipment

Sticks   Sticks must be made of wood or any other suitable material approved by the IHHF, such as aluminium or plastic. There must be no projections from the stick and the shaft must be straight.

The maximum length of the stick is 152cm (4ft 3in) measured from the heel to the end of the shaft. And the maximum length of the blade is 32cm (12½in) measured from the heel to the end of the blade. The blade should be between 5 and 7.5cm (2 and 3in) wide. All edges of the blade should be bevelled.

The goalkeeper's stick, however, is slightly larger, and the maximum width at any point is 9cm (3½in) except at the heel, where it can be 11.5cm (4½in). The length of the blade can be slightly larger also, at a maximum of 39 cm (15in).

An ice hockey skate.

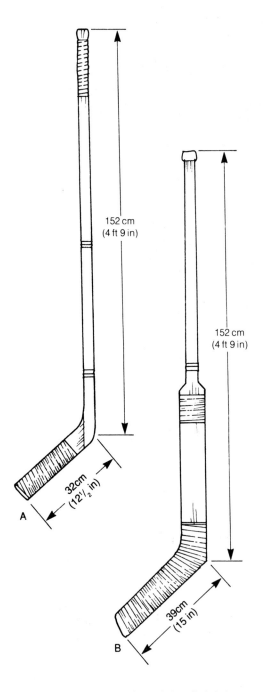

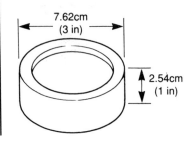

152 cm
(4 ft 9 in)

152 cm
(4 ft 9 in)

32cm
(12½ in)

39cm
(15 in)

A

B

The outfielder's stick, A, and the slightly larger goal keeper's stick, B.

Skates All skates, with the exception of the goalkeeper's, must be equipped with safety heel tips. The use of speed skates or any skate designed to cause injury is outlawed.

Puck The puck is made of vulcanized rubber or other approved material. It is 2.54cm (1in) thick and 7.62cm (3in) in diameter. It must be primarily black in colour. Its weight is 156–170gms (5½in–6oz).

7.62cm
(3 in)

2.54cm
(1 in)

The puck.

All players, including the goalkeeper, must wear the same outfit.

Players' uniforms

All the players of each team must be dressed uniformly and each must wear the same colour pants, stockings, sweater and helmet. Each player wears a number, which is at least 20cm (7¾in) in height, on the back of his sweater. No two players may be designated the same number. The team captain wears a letter 'C' on the front of his sweater. It must be in a contrasting colour and 8cm (3in) high.

Protective equipment

All players must wear a protective hockey helmet with a properly fastened chin-strap. Goalkeepers must wear a full face mask. Face masks are also compulsory in all IHHF sanctioned tournaments for players of 20 years of age and under. Players born after 1974 must wear visors. The face masks must be constructed in such a way that neither the puck nor the blade of the stick can penetrate it. Face masks are, however, recommended for all players.

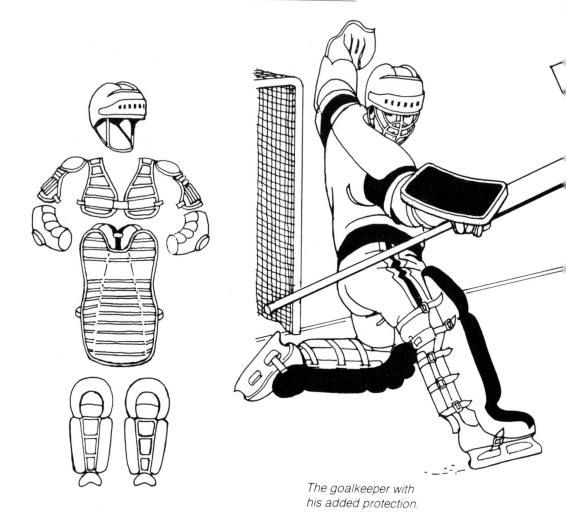

The goalkeeper with his added protection.

The protective clothing worn under the outfit.

Goalkeepers, because of the dangerous nature of their role, wear additional protective clothing, notably in the form of leg guards, larger gloves (as much to help them catch the puck as for protection), and leg, chest and arm protectors.

All protective equipment, with the exception of gloves, headgear, and goalkeepers pads, must be worn under the normal clothing.

That's ice hockey's equipment. And now for some terms which you will hear quite often as you play or watch the game, and ones that will appear regularly throughout this book.

Left to right: Nottingham Panthers – Ashley Tait and Paul Aley with Dean Edmiston of Edinburgh Racers

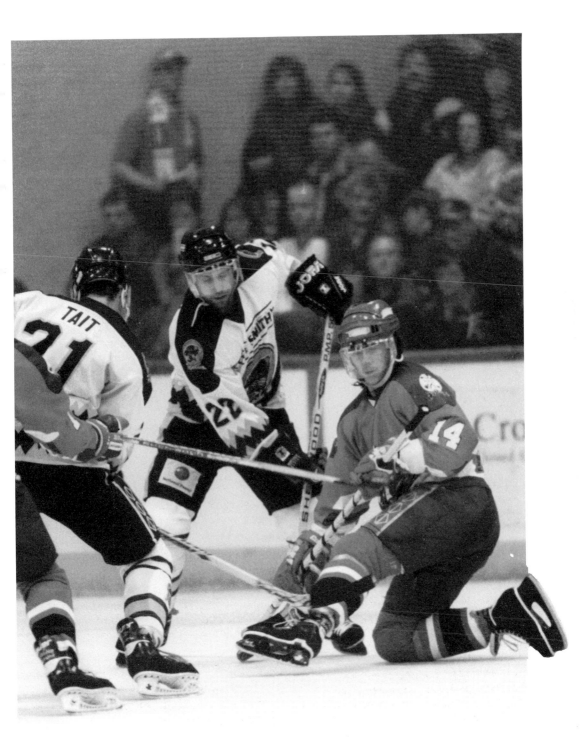

TERMINOLOGY

Altercation   Any physical interaction between two or more opposing players resulting in a penalty or penalties being awarded.

Assist   Up to two players may be credited with an assist when a goal is scored. An assist is awarded to the player who passed the puck to the scorer of the goal and to the player who passed it to the passer. Some goals are unassisted.

Back-checking   Forwards who to attempt to regain possession of the puck while skating towards their own goal are said to *backcheck*.

Bench penalty   The removal of a player from the game for two minutes following a breach of the rules. Any player of the team may serve the penalty, not necessarily the player who breached the rules.

Blind pass   A pass made without first looking up to see to whom the puck is going to be passed.

Board checking   The body-checking, cross-checking, elbowing, charging, or tripping of an opponent in such a way that he is thrown violently into the boards. Also known as *boarding*. If done illegaly, it incurs a penalty.

Boards   The boards surrounding the rink.

Breakaway   A quick forward motion out of defence, usually meaning that there are no defenders other than the goalkeeper between the attacking player(s) and the opposing goal.

Breaking pass   A pass to a team-mate who is accelerating ready for a breakaway.

Break-out   The movement of a team *en bloc* up the ice with the puck in its possession.

Boardchecking.

Butt-ending... using the end of the stick to impede an opponent.

Butt-ending   The illegal practice of using the shaft of the stick above the upper hand to jab or attempt to jab or impede an opposing player.

Cage   Another name for the goal, or goal cage.

Centre   The middle of the three attacking players, called 'forwards'.

Centre face-off circle   Another name for the centre circle. It is where the opening face-off is conducted, and every subsequent face-off after a goal.

Charging   Charging is deemed to have been committed if, in taking two steps or strides, a player runs, jumps into, or charges into an opponent, or body-checks or pushes an opponent from behind.

Check   Name given to the breaking up of an attacking move. It is the equivalent of a tackle in football.

Check back   Skating back towards your own goal to help out your defence.

Covering   Sticking close to an attacker thus preventing him from breaking away.

Charging.

Creases Areas marked out on the ice. There are three creases marked on the playing surface: two goalkeepers' creases, and a referee's crease. When play is stopped, for the award of a penalty, the referee may take up position in the referee's crease, and no player may enter it to argue with him.

Criss-cross attack The swapping of sides by the two wingmen during an attack.

Cross-checking Holding a stick with both hands to check an opponent by using the shaft of the stick with no part of the stick on the ice. It incurs a penalty.

Cross-over A skating move in which one foot is crossed over the other alternatively.

Cupping Illegally closing your hand on the puck.

Deke A dummy by the puck carrier to wrong-foot an opponent; a feint.

Delayed offside When an attacking player crosses the attacking blue line ahead of the puck but the defending team collects the puck and is in a position to bring it out of their defending zone without any delay or contact with an attacking player, the offside call is delayed. It is similar to the advantage rule in football.

Dig To attempt to win possession of the puck in the corners of the rink.

Cross-checking.

Directing the puck　The deliberate movement of the body, skate or stick with the intention of changing the direction of the puck.

Draw　The act of successfully getting the puck to a team-mate at a face-off.

Drop pass　Leaving the puck for a player behind to pick it up.

End zones　The two zones either side of the neutral zone.

Face-off　The means of starting play. The referee drops the puck between the two players involved in the face-off. The face-off ends when the puck has been legally dropped.

Flat pass　A pass in which the puck travels entirely along the ice.

Flip pass　A pass in which the puck is lifted so that it goes over an opponent or his stick.

Flip shot　A shot, more commonly forehand than backhand, in which the puck is flipped up towards the goal.

Forehand shot　A shot played on the left side by a right-handed player, and *vice versa*.

Freezing the puck　Holding the puck deliberately against the boards.

Game misconduct　If a player, coach or team manager receives a game suspension then he will be removed for the rest of the game and the offender will be ordered to the dressing room for the remainder of the game; but a substitute is permitted immediately.

The face-off

All players not involved in the face-off must be outside the circle, onside, and not within 4.5m (14ft 7in) of the players facing off.

Goal The only way of scoring a point in ice hockey, achieved when the *whole* of the puck crosses the goal-line and enters the net. It may not be kicked in with a skate deliberately, nor batted in with a glove, but it may deflect off a body. A goal scores one point.

Hard pass A pass made with a great deal of pace and force.

Heel of the stick That part of the stick between the straight part of the shaft and the flat part of the bottom of the blade.

High-sticking The carrying of a stick above the normal height of the shoulder is known as *high-sticking* and is prohibited.

Hip checking Using the hip to knock an opponent off stride.

Hooking Impeding an opponent by using the blade of the stick to pull or tug against his body or stick.

Icing the puck Icing the puck occurs when a player shoots the puck from his own half of the ice over the opposing goal-line, and it is then next touched by a defending player other than the goalkeeper. As soon the defending player touches the puck, play is stopped, and a face-off held in the other end zone. A team that is short-handed is allowed to ice the puck and there is no stoppage of play.

Interference Interfering with an opponent who is not in possession of the puck. Interference can be in the form of deliberately knocking the stick out of his hand, preventing him from recovering a dropped stick, or simply impeding his progress across the ice.

Last play face-off Face-off held at the spot where the puck was when it was last legally played immediately prior to a stoppage in play.

High sticks.

Left defenceman The person playing on the left side of defence.

Left wing Forward player on the left side.

Lift pass A pass made so that it lifts over any object or person that may be in the way.

Hooking.

Major penalty   A five-minute penalty, called for a major infraction of the rules.

Minor penalty   A two-minute penalty.

Misconduct penalty   A penalty resulting in a player being removed from the game for 10 minutes.

Neutral zone   The centre third of the playing area.

Offensive zone   The part of the playing area which houses your opponent's goal.

Off-ice officials   Also known as *minor officials*. They are the officials who are not positioned on the ice but play an important role in assisting the referee. They include the official scorer, game timekeeper, penalty timekeeper, and judges.

Off-the-board pass   A pass to a team-mate which is bounced off the boards.

Pass-out   A pass from an attacking player, when behind the opposing goal, to a team-mate in front of the goal.

Penalty   A penalty is awarded if a player or team official breaches any rules. The form the penalty takes varies according to the severity of the offence.

Penalty-killing   Defensive play of a team which, because of a penalty or penalties, has fewer players on the ice than its opponents have.

Penalty shot   A free skate and shot on goal. Only the goalkeeper can attempt to stop such a shot.

Interference.

Offside

A player is offside if he precedes the puck into the attacking zone. The determining factor is the position of the player's skates. Play is re-started from one of the face-off spots just outside the offending team's attacking zone.

Offside pass

The puck must not be passed over two lines (goal-line excepted), unless the puck precedes the receiving player over the middle red line. This is an offside pass and play re-starts from the face-off spot nearest to the point where the pass was made.

The pass-out

Player A passes out to team-mate B, who should have a shot at goal... defender (C) permitting.

Point   Position taken up by an attacking player, during a power play, just on or just inside the opponent's blue line (near the boards), to keep the puck from escaping from the opponents' end zone.

Possession of the puck   Any player, including the goalkeeper, who touches the puck is said to be in possession of the puck. A player is in possession even if the puck deflects off him or part of his clothing.

Possession and control of the puck   The last person to touch the puck and then control and propel it in a desired direction is said to be in possession and control of the puck.

Power play   Attacking play by a team which, because of a penalty or penalties, has a numerical advantage over its opponents. The object is to keep the puck inside the opponent's blue line by moving the whole team into the opponent's end zone.

Push pass   To move the puck up the ice with a shove rather than a full swing of the stick.

Right defenceman   The player who plays on the right side of the defence.

Right wing   Forward player on the right side.

Rink   The playing area.

Roughing   Any undue physical treatment of an opponent. It may earn either a minor or a major penalty.

Slashing.

Ace scorer Steve Moria in action

Stabbing with the point of the stick blade.

Rushing   A combined attack by some or all players of the team in possession of the puck.

Short-handed   A team is short-handed if it has more players on the penalty bench than its opponents have.

Sin bin   Slang term for the penalty bench.

Slap shot   Shot on goal made by raising the stick backwards and bringing it through the puck, somewhat in the manner of an abbreviated golf swing, in order to impart maximum force to the shot.

Slashing   The action of striking, or attempting to strike, an opponent with your stick. Striking your opponent's stick with your own is not slashing.

Slot   An imaginary area of the ice approximately 6–12m (20–40ft) in front of the goal.

Snap pass   A quick pass made with a snap of the wrists.

Spearing   Poking, or attempting to poke, an opponent with the top of the blade of your stick.

Spot pass   Pass in which the puck is sent to a pre-designated part of the rink rather than directly to a team-mate.

Stick-handling   The use of the stick to control and manoeuvre the puck while it is in one player's possession; similar to dribbling in football.

Substitute goalkeeper   A designated goalkeeper on the official score sheet who is not participating in the game.

Team official   Any person involved with the operation of a team. He may be the team director, manager, trainer, coach or even kit man.

Substitute goalkeeper   A player not designated as a goalkeeper can become a temporary goalkeeper if no goalkeeper or substitute goalkeeper is available. He assumes the benefits of a normal goalkeeper, but must re-assume his role as a 'player' if a designated goalkeeper is available.

Tripping   As its name implies, the tripping of an opponent. But it can be with either a stick, knee, foot, arm, hand, or elbow.

Tripping: ice hockey's most common penalty.

THE GAME –
A GUIDE

ce hockey is played by teams of six players on the ice at any one time, although teams consist of anything up to 20 players, all of whom may take part in a game. The replacement players must include one substitute goalkeeper.

Play is divided into three equal periods, each lasting 20 minutes. The time that the puck is actually in play is counted and the clock is stopped during any interruption in play. If the scores are level at the end of 60 minutes play then the game is declared a tie, unless the rules of the competition dictate that an extra period of 'overtime' has to be played until a winner is found. There is a 15-minute break between each period, and each team is allowed to take one 30-second **time-out** during the course of regular time or overtime.

The object of the game is to score more goals than the opposing team. It all sounds simple doesn't it? But, as with all sports, the simplified rules have hidden regulations which must be adhered to. So let's look a bit closer at the rules and the people who keep them.

THE · OFFICIALS

International matches are controlled by one referee and two linesmen who are assisted by a game timekeeper, a penalty timekeeper, an official scorer and two goal judges. But National Federations have the authority to use two referees instead of one referee and two linesmen.

Let's look closely at the specific roles of all the officials.

The referee   The referee has overall control and supervision of the other officials and the players. The referee's decision is **final**; so don't argue with him.

Referees and linesmen should wear black trousers and official sweaters which do not clash with either of the team's shirts.

When he goes on to the ice, the referee should have a whistle and a 2m (6ft 6in) tape measure in his possession. The tape measure is to enable him to measure a player's stick, if required to do so, to make sure it conforms with the rules.

As well as having overall control, the referee is responsible for the awarding of penalties and making decisions in case of disputed goals, but he can call upon the services of the linesmen or goal judges to help with such a decision. Don't forget, ice hockey is a fast game, and sometimes referees miss incidents. That's why they have other officials to help them.

The linesman   The linesman's chief duty is to determine when an offside or icing the puck has taken place. He is also responsible for stopping play when the puck goes out of the playing area or is interfered with by an ineligible person. He also calls a halt to the game if the puck is hit with the stick above shoulder-height or if a goal has been displaced from its original position.

Apart from the face-offs to start the game or a new period, or those after a goal has been scored, the linesman conducts all face-offs. However, he can be called upon at **any** time to perform one of the face-offs mentioned above if the referee so desires.

Above all, the linesman is there to help the referee to arrive at proper decisions and, when called upon for advice, he should be alert and quick to offer it.

Goal judges   There are two goal judges who are each positioned in a specially provided area situated behind each goal. Their job is to determine if the puck has completely crossed the goal-line and entered the net. In the British game, they also count the shots on goal.

Penalty box attendant   After awarding a penalty, the referee will announce the nature of the infringement, the player against whom the penalty is awarded, and the length of the penalty. This information is recorded by the penalty box attendant. He also notes in the Penalty Record the name of the player taking a penalty shot, and its outcome.

The penalty box attendant is responsible for making sure all penalties are duly served by offending players. He must also point out to the referee when one player receives his second *major* or *misconduct* penalty during a game.

Official scorer   Before the start of each game, the official scorer is handed a list of all eligible players and the starting line-up of each team by the appropriate coach or manager. This list is then, via the referee, made available to the opposing team.

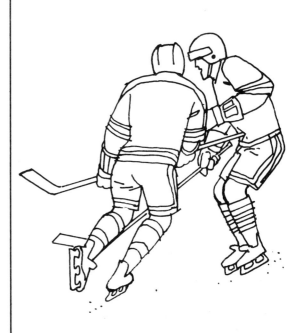

The scorer keeps a record of all goals, goalscorers, and players to whom assists have been credited, and makes a note of all players who actually take part in a game. He also notes the time that a substitute goalkeeper comes on to the ice. He also records penalty shots.

Game timekeeper   The timekeeper's role is to record the time of the start and finish of each game and all actual playing time. It is the timekeeper's responsibility to indicate the start of any period to the referee and it is the timekeeper who draws attention to the end of any period, or the match, by blowing a whistle, sounding a hooter, or using some other audible method.

If there is a public address system, he will announce when one minute remains of the first and second periods, and when there are two minutes left in the third period.

Should there be a dispute over the timing, the ultimate decision rests with the referee.

THE REFEREE'S SIGNALS

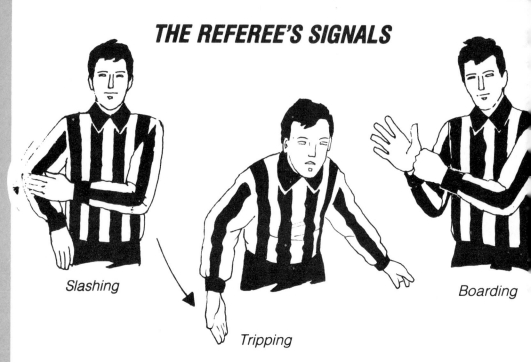

Slashing

Tripping

Boarding

Misconduct

Holding

Wash-o

cing

Interference

Elbowing

Hooking

Cross-checking

Charging

High-sticking

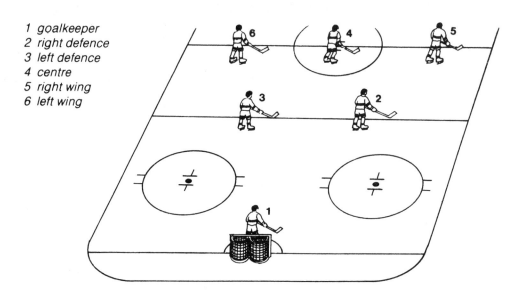

1 goalkeeper
2 right defence
3 left defence
4 centre
5 right wing
6 left wing

THE · PLAYERS

Teams consist of up to 20 members, but no more than six are allowed on the ice at any one time. The six players are as follows: goalkeeper; right defence; left defence; centre; right wing, and left wing.

Prior to the start of the game both teams give a list of all eligible players to the referee or official scorer, indicating their starting line-ups. The visiting team gives its line-up to the appropriate official first.

There must be no change to the line-up until the game has started. During the game players may be sent into play and taken off as often as the coach wishes to make changes, both during stoppages of play and while play is in progress.

THE · GAME

Starting of The Game

The game is started, and re-started, with a **face-off**.

Two opposing players stand squarely opposite each other facing their opponent's end of the rink, and approximately one stick-length apart. The blade of their sticks must be on the ice. The referee (or linesman) drops the puck on the ice between the sticks.

If the face-off takes place at one of the neutral or end zone face-off spots, then the players stand squarely facing each other and facing their opponent's end of the rink. Their sticks must be on the ice in contact with the designated white area. The player of the attacking team in *his* attacking half of the rink must place his blade on the ice first.

At a face-off, no other players are allowed in the face-off area and they must be standing up in an on-side position.

The face-off to start a game or each new period or to re-start after the scoring of a goal, takes place in the centre face-off area.

The home team has the choice of ends to defend in the first period; thereafter, ends are swapped at the beginning of each new period.

A superb shot of Pierre Turgeon in determined mood: head down, powering off his left leg and with that vital interception in mind.

However, if both team benches are on the same side of the rink then the home team defends the goal nearest its own bench first.

Moving the puck around the ice

Once the official places the puck on the ice at the face-off, the two players involved have to try to win possession of the puck. Thereafter, the puck is moved around the rink by passing and dribbling.

The puck is moved around the ice predominently with the blade of the stick. Kicking of the puck *is* allowed, but goals cannot be scored by kicking the puck into the goal. Neither can a goal be scored from a puck kicked and deflected into the goal off another player.

The puck can be passed among team-mates within one of the three zones, but it cannot be passed from a team's defensive zone to a team-mate on the opposite side of the centre red line, unless **the puck precedes the player across the line**. Otherwise it is offside.

Goals and assists

A goal is scored if the puck entirely crosses the goal line between the posts and under the crossbar of the goal. A member of the defending team can score an own goal, but credit for it is given to the last member of the attacking side to touch the puck. In the case of an 'own goal', no credit is given for an assist.

Pucks kicked into the goal do not, as we said earlier, count, nor do kicked pucks which are deflected off another player or goalkeeper. However, if a member of the attacking team hits the puck with his stick and it is deflected into the goal by either a member of his own team or the opposition, then the goal does count. If it is deflected by a team-mate, then *that* player is credited with the goal and the person making the shot gets credit for the assist.

After a goal is scored, an assist is credited to the player or players involved in the play immediately preceeding the goal but only two assists per goal are allowed. A player cannot receive credit for scoring and a for an assist in any one goal-scoring move. The purpose of recording assists is for record purposes only; they have no bearing on the score.

Unless the puck is in the goal crease, a member of the attacking side cannot enter this area, stand on the goal crease line, or have his stick in the crease. If he does, and subsequently scores a goal, it is not allowed and a face-off is held in the neutral zone face-off spot nearest the attacking zone of the offending team. However, if an attacking player is accidentally (or otherwise) pushed into the goal crease by a defending player, and a goal results, then it stands unless, in the opinion of the referee, the attacking player had time to get out of the crease.

Offside

A player is offside

(a) if he receives the puck from outside the opposing team's blue line when both his skates are inside the blue line (the stick *may* be inside the blue line)

(b) if he is standing inside the blue line when a team-mate carries the puck over that line into the opponents' zone.

(c) if, while standing in his opponent's end of the rink, with both his skates over the centre red line, he receives a puck that has been passed from behind his own blue line

An offside decision can be nullified if:

(a) the defending team passes or carries the puck into the neutral zone, or

(b) all attacking players in the attacking zone clear that sector.

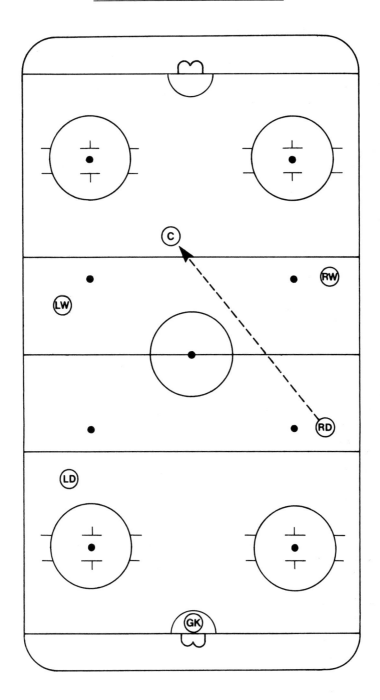

A player, C in this case, must not precede the puck into the attacking zone.

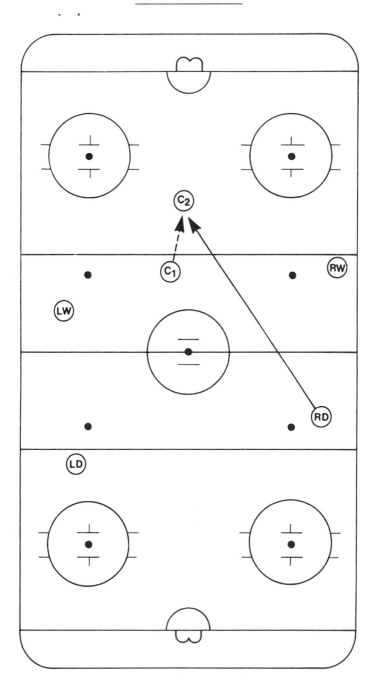

However, if RD made the pass when C was at position C1 and C gathered the puck at position C2 the pass is legal.

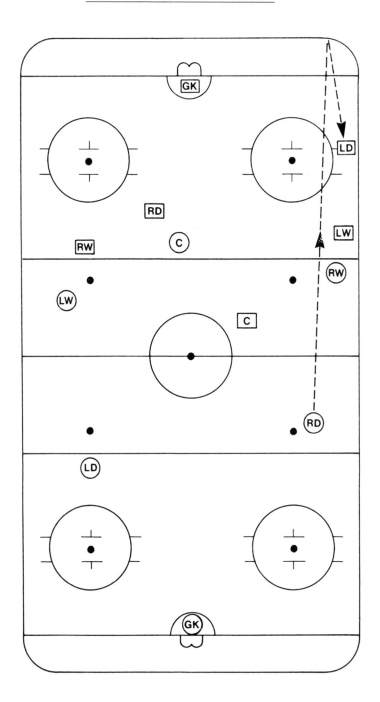

Icing the puck occurs if a player (RD in this case) plays the puck from his own half and the puck passes over the goal-line.

Icing the puck

Should any player shoot the puck from behind the centre red line beyond the opposing team's goal line the puck is declared **iced**. However, there are four instances when the puck cannot be iced:

(a) If the offending team is short-handed due to penalties;

(b) If the puck enters the net, in which case a goal will be awarded;

(c) If the puck crosses the goal-line direct from a face-off;

(d) If the puck touches, or in the opinion of the linesman, could have been played by a member of the opposing team, except the goalkeeper.

(e) if the puck touches any part of a member of the opposing team.

Once the puck has been iced, the referee halts the game and conducts a face-off at one of the face-off spots in the offending team's half of the rink.

Penalties

Because of the fast and furious nature of ice hockey there are many occasions when infringements, either deliberate or accidental, occur. The rules make provision for all of them whether they be major, minor, or obscure.

We shall look in greater detail at the more blatant infringements of the rules which bring about penalties, but first we will look at the six forms of penalty which can be awarded:

1. Minor penalty A player (other than a goalkeeper) is ruled off the ice for two minutes. No substitutes are allowed during that time. A goalkeeper's penalty is served by another member of his team.

2. Bench minor Like the minor penalty, a player is off the ice for two minutes (goalkeeper again excluded), but this time it need not necessarily be the offending player but can be another player of his team designated to serve the penalty by the manager or coach.

If a team is 'short-handed' by one or more players serving a minor penalty (or bench minor) and the opposing team scores a goal, then the penalty terminates immediately and the player can return to the ice.

3. Major penalty If a player (except a goalkeeper) is sent off the ice for a major penalty he shall be ruled of the ice for five minutes. Any subsequent major penalty against the same player rules him out of the remainder of the game, but a substitute is allowed to take his place after five minutes has elapsed.

4. Misconduct penalty For a misconduct penalty, a player (except a goalkeeper) is removed from the ice for ten minutes. However a substitute is allowed on the ice in his place immediately and the player serving the punishment is not allowed off the penalty bench until the first stoppage of play after the expiry of his ten-minute penalty.

5. Game misconduct penalty For such an offence, the player is removed from the ice immediately, is sent to the dressing room, and misses the remainder of the game. A substitute will, however, be allowed on the ice in his place immediately.

6. Gross misconduct penalty Any player or team official guilty of such an offence is removed from the match immediately and is not allowed to participate in another match until his case has been dealt with by the appropriate authority.

7. Match penalty A player is sent to the dressing room immediately and misses the remainder of the game. A substitute player is allowed to replace him but not until five minutes has elapsed.

Following the breach of any of the rules calling for a penalty shot (but not involving a major, misconduct, game misconduct, or match penalty), the non-offending team has the option of: (a) accepting the penalty shot, or (b) aving a minor penalty assessed against the ffending player. The latter gives the non-ffending team a numerical advantage over ieir opponents for two minutes.

If the penalty follows a breach that would npose a major, misconduct, game conduct or iatch penalty, then the penalty shot *must* be iken.

You will probably have noticed that, ɔalkeepers seem to be immune against being ent to the penalty bench. Well they are – to a ertain extent. They can, however, still commit ɔuls (and they do) and thus incur penalties ɔr their team.

If the goalkeeper commits a minor, major, or isconduct penalty, he will not be sent to the ɛnch. Instead, his time out of the game will be ɛrved by a team member who was on the ice t the time of the offence. However, should a ɔalkeeper receive two major penalties in one ame he will also receive a game misconduct ɛnalty. A game misconduct penalty against a ɔalkeeper involves his removal from the ame and his place is taken by the substitute ɔalkeeper. A match penalty against a 'keeper lso involves his removal from the game.

ʹenalty shot

, penalty shot is awarded when, in the idgement of the referee, a player who therwise had only the goalkeeper left to eat, has been prevented from attemping to :ore by any illegal interference, whether by player on the ice or by a player or official ff it.

The penalty shot is taken as follows:
The player designated to take the shot ∶ands alongside the centre face-off spot. he referee places the puck on the spot and n the referee's instruction the puck is layed from there in an attempt to score past ιe goalkeeper, who is the only person llowed to defend the penalty. Once the ᵤck is shot, the play is considered to be ompleted. No goal can be scored from a ɛcond shot, and once the puck crosses the ɔal-line the shot is deemed to be complete.

The goalkeeper must remain in his crease

until the penalty taker has touched the puck.

As to who takes the penalty, that is decided by the type of infringment in the first place. If it was awarded for any of the following:

(a) Deliberately displacing the goal during a breakaway;

(b) Hooking from behind;

(c) Interference;

(d) Illegal entry into the game;

(e) Throwing a stick, or

(f) Tripping from behind,

then the player fouled or involved in the incident takes the penalty shot. For any other infringement, the captain (or coach) of the non-offending team nominates a player to take the stroke.

During the playing of a penalty shot the ten players not involved stand at the side of the rink and behind the red centre line.

If a goal is scored, the resulting face-off is taken at the centre face-off circle. If the attempt is unsuccessful, the face-off is taken at one of the face-off spots in the end zone where the penalty shot was attempted.

Offences which can be penalized

Now that we have seen what the penalties are, we shall run through the list of offences that each of the penalties is awarded for.

Minor penalty

(a) Challenging or disputing the ruling of any official during a game. If you persist with such action, then expect your penalty to be 'upgraded' to a misconduct penalty.

(b) Causing the game to be held up for adjustment to your clothing.

(c) Not dropping a broken stick after it breaks. A player can play **without** a stick. If the goalkeeper's stick breaks he must carry on playing until play comes to a halt. He can then seek a replacement, but he must **not** leave his crease. It must be brought to him by a team-mate otherwise it is a minor penalty.

(d) Running, jumping or charging into an

opponent, or body-checking or pushing an opponent from behind. (This may also incur a major penalty, at the referee's discretion).

(e) A double minor (or major) will be imposed on a player who commits a foul on the goalkeeper inside the goal crease. This doesn't mean that you can foul a 'keeper once he's outside his area. You can't. Any unnecessary contact with the goalkeeper will still result in either a minor or major penalty at the referee's discretion.

(f) Making physical contact with a player after the whistle has blown if, in the opinion of the referee, the player had time to avoid such contact. At the referee's discretion he will award a minor or major penalty.

(g) Cross-checking an opponent results in either a minor or major penalty, again at the referee's discretion.

(h) Delaying the game by deliberately shooting, batting with the hand, or throwing the puck outside the playing area during a stoppage in play.

(I) Delaying the game by deliberately displacing the goal from its position. Play is immediately stopped if a goal is moved.

(j) Holding, freezing, or playing the puck along the boards in such a manner as to cause a stoppage in play.

(k) Using an elbow or knee to foul an opponent. This results in either a minor or major penalty, at the discretion of the referee.

(l) Deliberately falling on, or gathering, the puck into the body. This obviously doesn't apply to goalkeepers. If any other defending player should do so in the goal crease, a penalty shot is awarded and no other penalty given.

(m) Retaliating to fisticuffs. If after the initial retaliation persists and continues the altercation, the referee can award a double minor (four minutes) major, or match penalty.

(n) Closing a hand on the puck, by any player other than a goalkeeper. If a defending player picks up the puck in the goal crease, a penalty shot is awarded.

(o) Holding the puck by a goalkeeper for more than three seconds.

(p) Tripping an opponent with your stick, knee, foot, arm, hand or elbow.

(q) Deliberately dropping of the puck on the goal net by a goalkeeper.

(r) Carrying the stick above the normal height of the shoulder especially in a manner that endangers other players.

(s) Holding an opponent with your hands or stick. If you hold an opponent's face mask with your hand, the referee has the power to award a major penalty.

(t) Impeding an opponent by 'hooking' him with your stick.

(u) Interfering with, or impeding the progress of, an opponent not in possession of the puck. This also applies to interfering with the goalkeeper in the goal crease, unless the puck is already in that area.

(v) Impeding or attempting to impede an opponent by slashing him with your stick. This may be upgraded to a major if the referee feels it warrants it.

Bench minor

A bench minor will be awarded against a team if:

(a) A player fails to retire immediately to the penalty bench or dressing room when so ordered by the referee.

(b) A player or official uses foul, obscene or abusive language to any person while on the ice.

(c) A player, while off the ice, or a team official, prevents any official from carrying out his job properly.

(d) A team official bangs the boards.

(e) A team fails to place the correct number of players on the ice after a request to do so by the referee in order to get play under way.

lbowing.

lajor penalty

(a) If, as a result of body-checking, cross-hecking, elbowing, charging or tripping an pponent, he is forced violently into the oards, a major penalty may be awarded at ie referee's discretion, based upon the everity of the violence.

(b) Running, jumping, or charging into an pponent, or body-checking or pushing an pponent from behind, will result in a major or iinor penalty, at the referee's discretion.

(e) Committing a foul on the goalkeeper iside the goal crease will incur a major enalty or a double minor (four minutes). Any ther unnecessary contact with the oalkeeper results in either a major or minor enalty, at the referee's discretion.

(f) Making physical contact with a player fter the whistle has blown if, in the opinion of the referee, the player had time to avoid such contact. At the referee's discretion he will award a major or minor penalty.

(g) Cross-checking an opponent results in either a major or minor penalty, at the referee's discretion. Injuring an opponent as a result of cross-checking incurs a major penalty.

(h) Using the elbow or knee to foul an opponent results in either a minor or major penalty, at the discretion of the referee. If a player is injured as a result of a foul committed with the elbow or knee, a major is awarded.

(i) Injuring an opponent as a result of carrying a high stick or hooking. ('Injuring' means that blood is drawn.)

(j) Holding an opponent's face mask (it can be downgraded to a minor, at the referee's discretion.)

(k) Impeding, or attempting to impede, an opponent by slashing. This may be downgraded to a minor at the referee's discretion, but if you injure an opponent as a result of slashing, it is automatically a major. Swinging your stick at another player during an altercation is also a major, or possibly a match penalty.

Misconduct penalty

A player may have a misconduct penalty awarded against him for any of the following offences:

(a) Using obscene or abusive language to any person on the ice or anywhere in the rink before, during, or after the game, except in the immediate vicinity of the players' bench.

(b) Deliberately knocking the puck out of reach of an official who is retrieving it.

(c) Deliberately throwing any equipment out of the playing area.

(d) Banging the board with a stick, or other instrument.

(e) Failing to proceed immediately to the penalty bench when so instructed by the referee.

(f) Inciting an opponent into incurring a penalty after receiving a warning against such behaviour from the referee.

(g) Entering the referee's crease while he is talking to another official. However, a player may have to enter the crease to get to the penalty bench, in which case this is permitted.

(h) Body-checking, tripping, or holding with stick or hands any game official.

(i) Continuing to fight or being involved in an altercation after being told to stop by the referee.

(j) Getting involved in fisticuffs when off the ice. However, if one player is off the ice and one on it then both are deemed to be 'on' for the purpose of this rule and can therefore receive a match penalty at the referee's discretion.

Goal! Scott Neil defeats Humberside Hawks' goalie Danny Thompson

(k) Spearing, attempting to spear, butt-ending, or attempting to butt-end an opponent carries a misconduct penalty against the offending player in addition to a minor or major penalty which the referee will award at his discretion

NOTE: (h), (i), (j) and (k) can incur either a misconduct, or a game misconduct, penalty, at the referee's discretion.

Game misconduct penalty

Any player found guilty of the following may be awarded a game misconduct penalty:

(a) Persisting in any conduct for which a misconduct penalty has already been awarded.

(b) Using obscene gestures anywhere on the ice either before, during, or after a game. Any team official found guilty of any type of misconduct shall be given a game misconduct penalty.

Gross misconduct penalty

The following offences result in a gross misconduct penalty being awarded:

(a) Any conduct which interferes with, or is detrimental to, the smooth running of the game. This applies to players and team officials.

(b) Any attempt deliberately to injure, an official during a game.

Match penalty

A match penalty may be imposed for:

(a) Attempting deliberately to injure an opponent, especially by spearing or butt-ending.

(b) Starting fisticuffs.

(c) Kicking, or attempting to kick, an opponent.

(d) Swinging your stick at an opponent during an altercation.

Miscellaneous infringements

If any object is thrown on to the ice from anywhere in the rink, the following penalties are awarded:

(a) If thrown by a player, he is given a minor penalty, plus a game misconduct penalty.

(b) If thrown by a team official, he is given a game misconduct penalty and his team awarded a bench minor against it.

(c) If thrown by an unidentified person of the team in the vicinity of the player's bench, then that team is assessed a bench minor penalty.

Finally we ought to look at the rules concerning throwing a stick.

If a player, goalkeeper, or team official deliberately throws a stick (or other object) in the direction of the puck in the defending zone the referee will allow play to continue. If a goal is not scored, then he will award a penalty shot and designate the player who he deemed to be fouled to take the shot.

If the player attacking had an unattended goal to aim at and the puck was interfered with by an object thrown on to the ice, thus preventing the shot at the open goal, then the referee will award a goal.

A major penalty is awarded against any player or goalkeeper who throws his stick, or other object, on to the ice irrespective of which zone the puck is in at the time. However, if a penalty shot is awarded, or a goal scored, then the major penalty is not awarded.

Well, if you want to still play ice hockey after that lot then good luck!

There are a lot of possible infringements of the rules. But, as we said earlier, the game is so fast that the rules must make provision for every contingency. However, the most important rule to remember is the one about common sense. Ice hockey really is a simple game, not that you would think so by the list of rules. However, despite outlining the list of **do's and dont's**, there are still some finer points of the rules that need clearing up and we will do that in a questions and answers format in the next chapter.

RULES

CLINIC

You said that the visiting team must first give its starting line-up to the referee before a game begins, then followed by the home team. But what happens if the game is played at a neutral venue?

Then the 'home' team will be decided by the loss of a coin or some other method.

What happens if both goalkeepers of one team are unable to continue because of injury or their removal from the game. Can another player take over in goal?

Yes. A team will be allowed ten minutes to prepare another player. But once he has taken to the ice, neither of the original goalkeepers can return to the game.

Can penalties be incurred after the conclusion of a game?

Yes. While players are still on the ice, they are liable to be penalized for any infraction of the rules.

Obviously a player can receive a major and minor penalty at the same time. Which penalty does he serve first?

The major penalty.

What happens if a player has a minor (or major) and a misconduct penalty against him?

The player shall serve the misconduct penalty of ten minutes and a substitute team-mate shall accompany him on the penalty bench to serve the minor (or major) penalty. The substitute returns to the ice after the two minutes (or five) of the lesser penalty have been served.

If a player receives a game misconduct penalty, is he automatically suspended by the League or Association for a certain number of games?

No. The suspension is not automatic. However, the matter is reported to them and they have the powers to suspend a player if they so desire.

What further penalty is imposed on a player receiving a match penalty?

He shall be barred from playing in all future games until his case has been heard and dealt with by the appropriate authority.

You said that in certain circumstances, the player involved in an incident resulting in a penalty shot has to take the shot. But what happens if he is unable to take the shot due to injury?

Then his team captain (or coach) will nominate another player, who was on the ice at the time of the incident, to take the shot in his place.

OK! So what happens if the player who has the penalty shot awarded to him also commits a foul which would result in him being sent to the penalty bench? Does he stay on the ice to take the shot?

Yes. But he then retires to the bench.

If, while taking a penalty shot, a player is distracted by a member of the opposing team, what action is taken?

If a goal is scored it stands. If not, and the referee feels that the action prevented a goal, then the penalty is re-taken and the offending player receives a misconduct penalty for interfering or distracting.

Is the time required for a penalty shot included in normal time?

No.

Because goalkeepers are not required to serve some penalties, does this mean that, for record purposes, they didn't commit the foul?

No. Even though their 'sentence' is served by a team-mate, they are still credited with the penalty.

Despite the strange situation, both Sheffield Steelers' Tim Cranston and Cardiff Devils' Milton Ruggles are still reaching for the puck!

What happens if a team has two players on the penalty bench and another player receives his 'marching orders'?

That player also goes to the bench and he is replaced by a substitute player thus making sure the team has four men on the ice. However, when one of the original two men serving their penalty returns to the game, the substitute leaves the ice and the third player's penalty period starts.

If a player commits two or more penalties on the same play does he serve the penalties simultaneously or consecutively?

Consecutively.

You said that a minor penalty is awarded against a player who deliberately displaces the goal. Surely, it would be worth risking a minor penalty to move the goal during the course of a breakaway from the opposing team to prevent them scoring?

Not very sporting I must say! However, the rules allow for people with devious minds like that and a penalty shot is awarded, to be taken by the person last in possession of the puck at the time of the offence. A penalty shot is also awarded if you deliberately hook, or trip, or interfere with a player in control of the puck and on the attacking side of the red centre line and with no opponents, other than the goalkeeper, to beat.

Can a player carry the puck into his own defensive zone when he is in fact outside the zone?

Yes and No ... No, he cannot do it as a means of wasting time, like the back pass in soccer. However, if his team is numerically under strength then **yes** he is allowed to enter his own defensive zone with the puck, but deliberately delaying the game is still not allowed.

Can a goal be scored if the puck is deflected off an official into the goal net?

No.

When discussing the offside rule you said a player cannot precede the puck into the attacking zone. Does this mean that a player in possession of the puck cannot enter the zone before the puck?

No. The rules allow for a player in control of the puck to enter the attacking zone ahead of the puck.

What exactly determines a player's position for the purpose of the offside rule?

The position of his skates. Both skates must be completely over the line. His stick may be over the line so long as one of his skates is not.

Can a pass be made from your own defensive zone to a player over the half-way line?

No, unless the puck precedes the receiving player across the red line. However, the receiving player can stand in the attacking half of the rink and retreat to touch the red line with either skate and then gather the ball. This is permitted, but he has to be quick to do that!

What happens if the puck goes out of bounds and off the playing area?

There will be a face-off near to the point where it was shot or deflected before going out of bounds.

TECHNIQUES

The position of the hands on the stick for normal stick-handling.

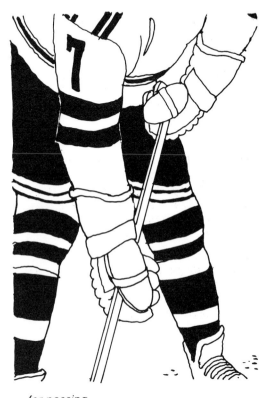

... for passing.

THE BASICS

Holding the stick

The first thing you need to learn is how to hold the stick correctly.

The stick is held with the fingers, not the palm, of the hand. It is held between your forefinger and thumb, with the thumb applying pressure to hold it in place. The left hand (if you are a right-handed player) is the one placed furthest down the stick. The right hand supports it near to the top.

For normal stick-handling, the left hand should be approximately 38–45cm (15–18in) from the top of the stick. It should be about 15cm (6in) lower when passing and another 15cm (6in) lower when shooting.

Don't skate with your stick in the air. Hold it close to the ice and ready to put on to the

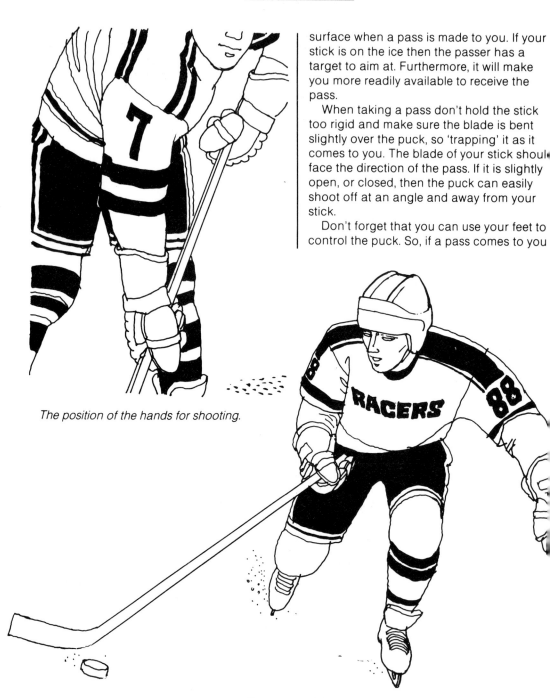

surface when a pass is made to you. If your stick is on the ice then the passer has a target to aim at. Furthermore, it will make you more readily available to receive the pass.

When taking a pass don't hold the stick too rigid and make sure the blade is bent slightly over the puck, so 'trapping' it as it comes to you. The blade of your stick should face the direction of the pass. If it is slightly open, or closed, then the puck can easily shoot off at an angle and away from your stick.

Don't forget that you can use your feet to control the puck. So, if a pass comes to you

The position of the hands for shooting.

Keep your stick on, or close to, the ice ready to accept the pass.

TECHNIQUES

Always be prepared to improvise when you have possession of the puck.

It is okay to control the puck with your foot... even though you can't score by kicking the puck into the goal.

unexpectedly and you can't control it in time with your stick, use your feet to control the puck before taking over with your stick.

Skating practice

There is a lot more to ice hockey than just having the ability to receive and pass the puck, and shooting. Don't forget the game is played on **ice**; so you need to be able to skate well.

You need the ability to turn quickly, make cross-overs, and stop and start on the ice. Just because you can skate, it doesn't mean you will automatically become a proficient ice hockey player.

Practice is essential in any sport, and ice hockey is no different. You need to practise your skating skills as well as your playing skills. And in between matches you should try the following workouts on your own. An excellent stop-start routine is as follows:

And don't forget that you are allowed to handle the puck. You can't hold it, but you can stop a puck travelling through the air and bat it down, so long as you don't pass it forwards. You can't direct the puck to a team-mate with your hand.

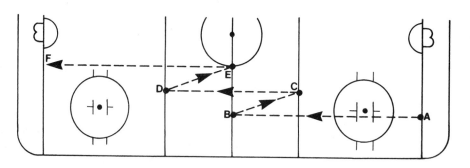

A good exercise for practising your stopping and starting;

Skate forward from A to B, then backwards to C, forward to D backwards to E, and finally forward to F. Make your turns fluently and quickly.

And this is what the quick
turn looks like in a match
situation.

(a) Skate at speed from a goal-line to the
centre line.

(b) Stop, turn and skate back to the first
blue line.

(c) Stop, turn and skate over the centre-line
to the next blue line.

(d) Stop, turn and skate back to the centre
line.

(e) Stop, turn and skate at speed to the
opposing goal-line.

Repeat this exercise several times. Speed is not
essential initially. It is important, however, that
you make sure your stops and turns are clean.
Once you have perfected them, then the speed
element will come automatically.

If practised in a team group, the exercise
can be treated as a relay race by dividing the
players into two groups.

A variation of the above is the shuttle, in
which a skater (or skaters) starts skating up
the rink at speed and the coach or trainer
blows a whistle. Once blown, the player has to
stop, turn and skate in the opposite direction.

Every time the whistle is blown the player has
to change direction. Listen out for the quick
whistles in rapid succession ... believe me, he'll
give you a few of them.

To practise cross-overs, you should start in
the middle of the rink and skate in a figure-of-
eight around the back of the goals. You
should get used to skating at speed and
taking sharp turns at the corners.

Practice can be fun, and it **should** be fun.
You mustn't shun practice. It is very important
in making you not only a better player, but a
better individual. The discipline of practice is
good for your discipline when you get out onto
the ice to play a match.

There are many other forms of practice,
besides the couple outlined above. But you
will, more often than not, find yourself involved
in team practice and training, rather than
practising on your own. Consequently, your
team coach will have his own schedule
worked out for you.

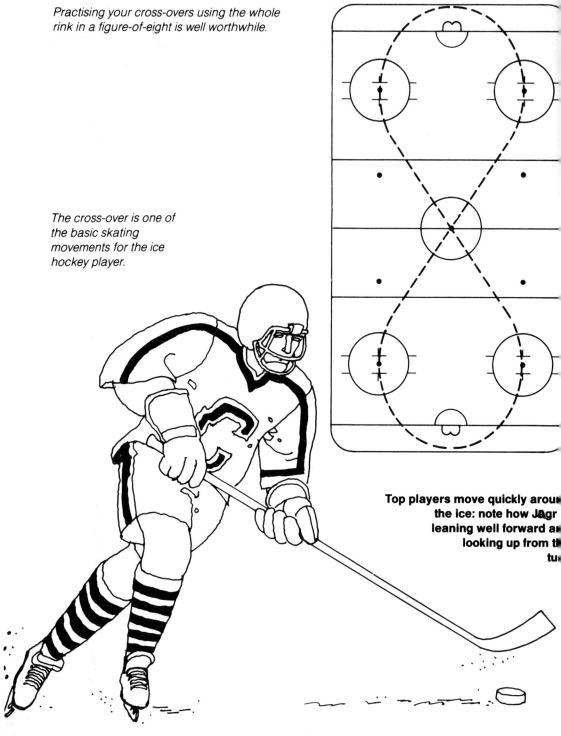

Practising your cross-overs using the whole rink in a figure-of-eight is well worthwhile.

The cross-over is one of the basic skating movements for the ice hockey player.

Top players move quickly arou
the ice: note how Jagr
leaning well forward a
looking up from t
tu

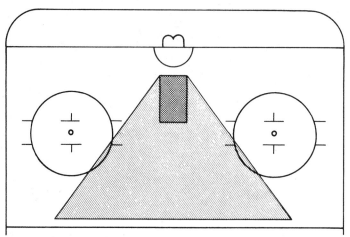

 Represents 'the slot'... the prime shooting area.

Represents the next-best shooting area.

When the goalkeeper takes up his position on the goal-line he doesn't leave you much of the target to aim at.

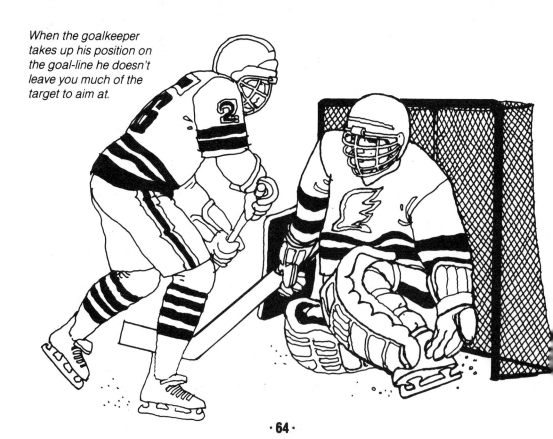

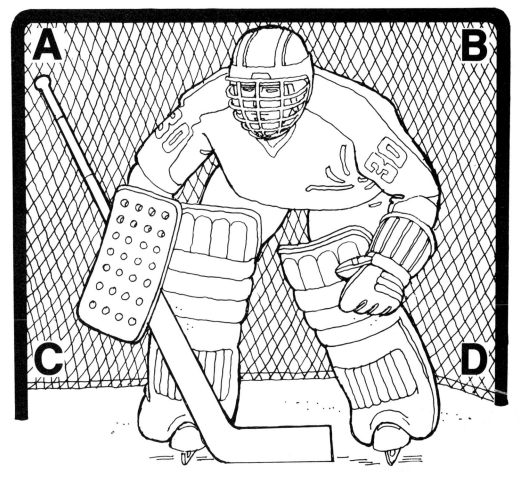

The four most vulnerable areas of the goal... as far as the 'keeper is concerned that is!

PLAYING SKILLS

Right, now it's time to look at some playing skills. First, let's get to know the vital attacking areas of the rink.

Key shooting areas

The prime shooting area is that small area 3 to 7.5m (10 to 24ft) immediately in front of the goal. It is known as the **slot**. The area extending in front of the goal in a triangle shape is deemed to be the next most advantageous shooting area. But after that it really is no-hopers land. Very rarely do you see

long-distance goals in ice hockey. Most are scored from close in around the slot and from a position directly in front of the goal.

Most goalkeepers have a weak and strong side. In the majority of cases the strong side is the one adjacent to their free hand. Therefore, you should aim your shot to the opposite side of the goal, the side containing the 'keeper's stick-holding hand.

Shots to either the top or bottom corners of the goal are the most difficult for the goalkeeper to stop.

The most common shot is the **wrist shot**. The stick is swept along the ice and the shot

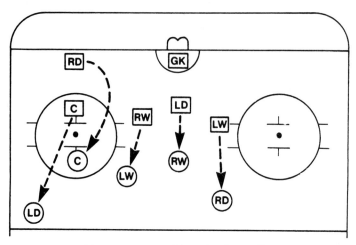

Man-to-man marking at a face-off...
possible positions.

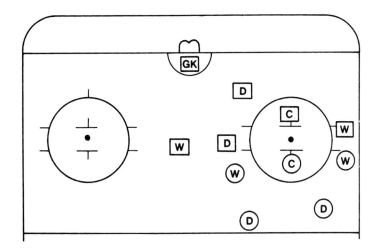

Taking quick advantage of possession at the
face-off is crucial. It is therefore important to
set up a good positional line-up, depending
upon position of face-off. It also depends
whether the face-off man is right- or left-
handed. In this example the attacking face-off
man, C, is left-handed. Note how the defence
takes up their positions knowing the puck is
likely to head towards the goal.

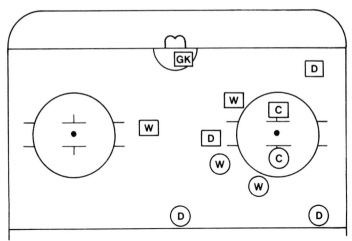

... And a possible positional line-up for a right-handed attacking face-off man (C).

Position of players at a face-off when one is left-handed and the other right-handed.

made with a quick snap of the wrist at the last moment before contact.

The face-off

At a face-off, only the two players involved, plus the referee or linesman, are allowed in the face-off circle. All other players must be outside the circle and in an onside position.

Positioning of the other players at the face-off is important, and it is equally important that the player involved in the face-off is aware of the positioning of his team-mates because he wants to try and gain possession of the puck and direct it towards one of them. The placing of players outside the circle must also take into consideration whether one of the players involved in the face-off is right- or left-handed. It is a bit like placing the fielders in cricket; they take up different positions depending upon the batsman being right- or left-handed.

The face-off.. a player's view.

The goalkeeper

Before we look at some attacking plays, we ought to look at the role of this key player.

Because of the dangerous nature of the game, and the goalkeeper's job in particular, he is well padded and protected against the dangers of the sport. The puck is constantly being hit at him at speeds of around 100mph (160kph).

The goalkeeper has to be very agile, and

fearless. He must also have the ability to read the game and be aware of where all players are at all times.

A good goalkeeper does not only prevent goals from being scored, but is also an inspiration to his team and, in fact, plays his part in setting up goals for his colleagues.

The ability of a goalkeeper to narrow the angle of an incoming forward is of paramount importance. The goal may not seem very large when the goalkeeper is

But, of course, it is not that easy. The other team will be applying pressure in the hope of regaining possession or forcing an error.

When a defender is pressurized by an attacker, the **peel-off** is a useful ploy. The puck is played off the boards at an angle that will get it away from the checkers and towards a team-mate, who can then set up an attack.

Often you will see a defender play a long diagonal pass across the ice to his opposite wing. This pass is best made by rebounding the puck off the boards to take the pace off the puck. But a good sound knowledge of the boards is important when playing such a pass. When the pass is successful it is very effective.

The 'one-two' is another good form of break-out play. The defender plays the puck to a wingman who retreats to gather the puck. As he is doing that, the defender skates up the ice to collect the return pass and start the attacking move.

But don't forget, while one team is trying to work a break-out play, the other team will be trying to prevent a break-out. A typical checking move would be for the centre to protect the area in front of the goal and for one winger to move down the boards while the other covers the middle of the attacking zone. But their exact positions, of course, depend on the position of the puck-carrier.

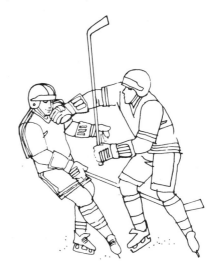

standing in it, but don't forget that the puck isn't all that big either and can easily creep through the gaps left by the 'keeper. He must therefore give the attacker as little of the goal to see as possible when making a shot.

Break-out plays

The defence will often win possession of the puck in their own defensive zone and will have to work it up the ice for the forwards.

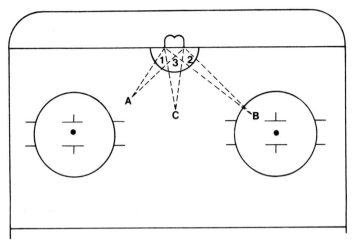

Goalkeepers should narrow the angle to give the attacker less of the goal to aim at. If the attacker is at position A then the 'keeper should be at position 1. If the attacker is at B then the 'keeper should be at 2, and at 3 if the attacker is at position C.

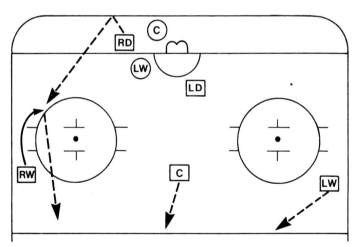

RD is closely marked. But he can get out of trouble by playing the puck off the boards to RW, who retreats back, collects the puck and builds up an attack with C and LW.

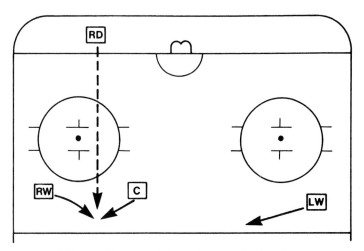

RD can effect a quick break-out to RW or C...

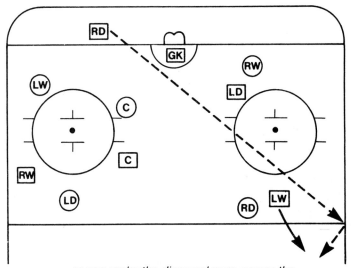

...or can make the diagonal pass across the ice, and off the boards, to LW. The puck has crossed two lines but as one of them is the goal-line it cannot be an offside pass.

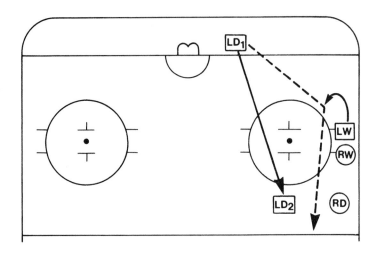

The 'one-two' pass. LD1 passes to LW who retreats to get away from his checker. LD moves to position LD2 and collects the return pass.

Doug Gilmour has possession of the puck: note how he is already looking ahead and moving off. Norwich Union final, Birmingham 1988/89; Durham Wasps v Dundee Tigers

TECHNIQUES

Passing

When passing, always be aware where the puck is going. Don't pass just for the sake of getting rid of it, since that will achieve nothing and probably give the puck to an opponent. Always pass to a team-mate, or away from an opponent, and always be aware of what the result of your pass will be. And whatever you do, **don't** pass the puck in front of your own goal. It is inviting the opposition to intercept and score.

If you get the puck close to the side of your own goal, try and work the puck up the ice and beyond your own blue line before passing. Don't pass it from the goal to the centre of the ice. The interception can, once more, be made and you will probably not have time to recover. So, bring the puck forward and when you see a team-mate better placed than you, make the pass to him.

Having broken out from defence, it is now time to set up an attacking play.

If you gather the puck close to your own goal, look up and see where your team-mates and opponents are positioned. Rather than making the pass, try to move the puck up the ice.

Attacking plays

The important thing to remember about attacking play is to make sure you get one of your attackers into the **slot**. More often than not the centre will attack the slot, but various manoeuvres can see any of the forwards taking up position in the slot.

One powerful play involves the two wings attacking the goal with the centre staying in the slot. This puts a lot of pressure on the goalkeeper and defence.

It is equally harrassing for the defence if one of the wingers and the centre attack the goal while the other winger moves in to take up position in the slot.

Another good attacking play that will probably cause confusion among the defence is for one wing to stay close to the boards, and the other to either do the same, or attack the goal. The centre then attacks the slot, but his position will depend upon where the 'floating' wings decide to make their attack – either down the boards or to the net.

Once you are in your opponent's attacking zone, don't pass the puck the width of the rink if they have a player capable of reaching the puck and making the interception. That will give the defence the chance of a breakaway.

ICE · HOCKEY

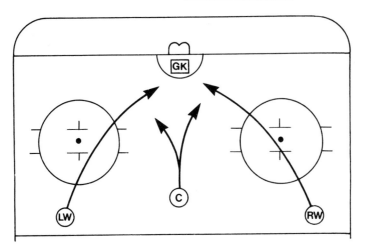

An attacking move with the two wings attacking the goal and the centre occupying the slot.

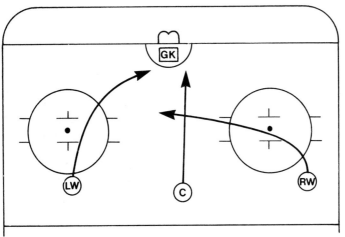

This time the left wing (LW) and centre (C) attack the goal and right wing (RW) makes a move to the slot.

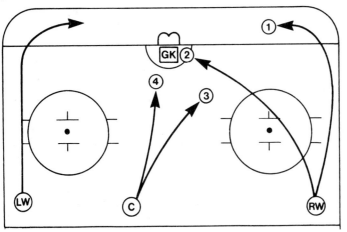

LW moves down the boards and C takes up his attacking position depending upon RW's move.. if to 1, then C moves to 3. If RW moves to position 2, then C goes to 4.

TECHNIQUES

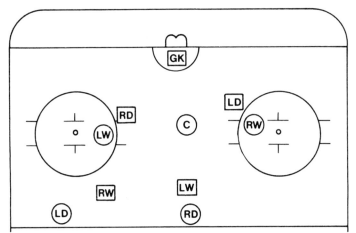

If you are a man short, you should make sure you cover your team-mates when on the defensive, as shown.

You must always support your team-mates whether they are on the offence or defence. Once you have advanced up the ice and shot, or passed, then you must remain aware of what is happening and be ready to take possession of the puck for another attack, or to defend if appropriate.

Often during a match you will find your team is either playing with a numerical advantage or disadvantage because of players sent to the penalty bench.

In the case of the former, you need to try to capitalize on having a man (or two) more than the opposition and apply as much pressure by way of constant attacks during your period of numerical advantage. Even if you don't score during the period, you will probably tire your opponents out a bit more than normal. And tired players eventually make mistakes.

If you are numerically *inferior* to your opponents because you have a player or players on the penalty bench, you will be on the receiving end of such pressure and you and your team-mates must know how to handle such a situation when the opposing team attacks.

The important thing is to try and prevent a goal, or a shot at goal, and this is where clever covering is called for. Don't stand too close to either the puck-carrier, or any other opposing players, but stand well off so that if you or a

colleague is beaten, you can quickly cover. Ice hockey is too fast a game to show you typical plays. It is impossible to play the game according to a textbook. You only have to get out there to realize you don't have time to stop and think about what you are going to do next. You certainly have to **think** about what you do, but as for stopping, I'm sorry but there won't be time!

The word **quickly** has appeared quite a lot, but it is an important word in ice hockey, as you will have realized. You have to think, react, move, and pass and shoot **quickly**.

It doesn't matter whether you are attacking, defending, breaking-out or keeping goal. You have to be able to react quickly to every situation. Do that and you will become a proficient player. However, when you first start, be patient, and don't forget that everybody started at the same place as you.

We emphasized earlier the need to practise. We will close on the same subject.

Throughout the entire *Play the Game* series we have pointed out that we cannot turn you into an outstanding prospect. Only **you** can do that. And the best way to do that is by training and practising regularly. You must have the **desire** to become a better player. If you have that desire then you are a long way towards achieving your aim.

USEFUL
ADDRESSES

USA Hockey Inc
4965 North 30th Street
Colorado Springs
CO 80191, USA
Tel: (001 719) 599 5500
Fax: (001 719) 599 5994

British Ice Hockey Association
Second Floor Suite
517 Christchurch Road
Boscombe
Bournemouth
BH1 4AG
Tel: (01202) 303946
Fax: (01202) 398005

Canadian Amateur Hockey League
1600 Promenade
James Naismith Drive
Gloucester
Ontario, Canada
K1B 5N4
Tel: (001 613) 748 5613
Fax: (001 613) 748 5709

International Ice Hockey Federation
Todistrasse 23
CH-8002
Zurich
Switzerland
Tel: (00 41) 281 1430

National Hockey League
1800 McGill College Ave
Suite 2600
Montreal
Quebec N3A 3J6
Canada
Tel: (001 514) 288 9220
Fax: (001 514) 284 0300

Goalie John Vanbiesbrouck is making good use of feet, pads and stick in guarding the goal but is still poised to drop to the ice if needed

RULES CLINIC

INDEX

INDEX

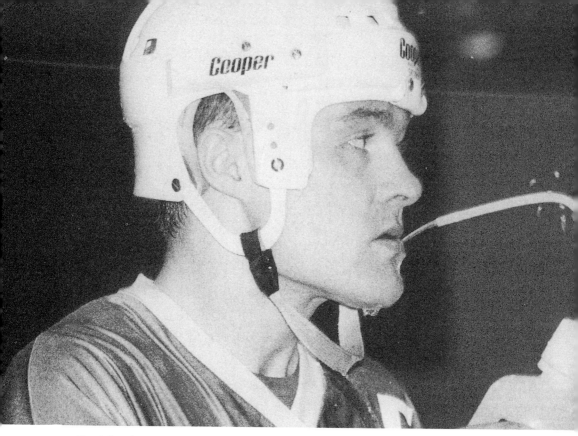

Captain of Durham Wasps, Great Britain International Paul Smith